SCHIRMER PERFORMANCE EDITIONS

HAL LEONARD PIANO LIBRARY

J.S. BACH
TWO-PART INVENTIONS

Edited and Recorded by Christopher Taylor

T0195172

To access companion recorded performances online, visit:
www.halleonard.com/mylibrary

Enter Code
1674-7475-7383-9651

On the cover:
Interior of St. Peter's, Rome
by Giovanni Paolo Pannini
(1691-1765)
© Bridgeman Art Library, Getty Images

ISBN: 978-0-634-07359-5

G. SCHIRMER, Inc.

DISTRIBUTED BY

HAL•LEONARD®
CORPORATION
7777 W. BLUEMOUND RD. P.O. BOX 13819 MILWAUKEE, WI 53213

www.musicsalesclassical.com
www.halleonard.com

CONTENTS

The price of this publication includes access to companion recorded performances online, for download or streaming, using the unique code found on the title page. Visit **www.halleonard.com/mylibrary** and enter the access code.

HISTORICAL NOTES

BACH AS MUSIC TEACHER

When Johann Sebastian Bach (1685-1750) wrote fifteen short pieces to encourage his ten-year-old son's facility with keyboard playing and composition, he could hardly have anticipated the appeal they would hold around the world nearly three centuries later. Having been born into a large family of professional musicians in central Germany, Bach was surrounded by music his whole life, and he personally ensured that his children would become musicians.

Bach's own childhood was marked by the tragic loss of both parents within a year at the tender age of nine. Once orphaned, he moved in with his newly married brother Christoph, an organist in a nearby town. After graduating from boarding school, Bach bypassed a University education in order to work as an organist, court and chamber musician, and later Kapellmeister in various Thuringian towns. In 1723, he finally settled in Leipzig as Cantor at the St. Thomas School (where students were aged 12-23). Although professional frustrations abounded in Leipzig, he remained there until his death in 1750.

When Bach applied for the prestigious post at the St. Thomas School, competition was tight, and he was by no means assured of the job. His growing fame as an organist, concertmaster, and composer certainly would have impressed the school; however, Bach had to prove his skills as a schoolteacher, since he lacked formal experience in that area. To that end, he produced some clearly didactic works, which he likely submitted to the St. Thomas committee: *The Well-Tempered Clavier* (Book I), a book of organ instruction, and the *Aufrichtige Anleitung* ("Upright Instruction"). The 15 two-part Inventions comprised half of the *Aufrichtige Anleitung*; the three-part Sinfonias made up the other half. The Inventions were a revised version of the *Praeambula* Bach had written for his son Wilhelm Friedemann's *Clavier-Büchlein* (Little Piano Book) three years earlier.

In his preface to the publicly available version of the Inventions and Sinfonias, Bach indicates that the pieces should help students to develop a *cantabile* (singing) style and to acquire a strong foretaste in composition. Musical analysis, even at a rudimentary level, remains fundamental to learning the inventions. A short, identifiable idea (*inventio*) appears in each voice; then ideas recur, whole or fragmented, and are occasionally inverted (the inversion being a mirror image of the motive). With each Invention written in a different key, the student can become familiar with how various keys feel to the hands, while simultaneously learning to read a variety of key signatures.

As mentioned earlier, Bach successfully obtained the post in Leipzig, and as a result, teaching became a defining activity for the remainder of his life. He was surrounded by students and colleagues at St. Thomas, and university students sought private study with this renowned keyboard virtuoso and master of counterpoint. Many of his students became important musicians or followed such academic pursuits as law, medicine, or philosophy. Bach's own sons, whose educations he closely monitored, became the first generation in the family to complete university training.

Before Bach's music became known to the general public in the 19th century, his devoted students (and, in turn, their pupils) had already recognized Bach as their exemplar. To this day, he remains a central figure for teachers, students, and audiences of Western music. Nearly every serious piano student is introduced to Bach through the two-part Inventions, 15 delightful little pieces that started life modestly as exercises to educate and entertain Bach's talented children.

—*Denise Pilmer Taylor*

PERFORMANCE NOTES

On the title page of his autograph copy of the Inventions and Sinfonias Bach placed the following description:

> Honest method by which lovers of the keyboard—especially those eager to learn—are shown a way not only (1) to learn to play cleanly in two parts, but also, after further progress, (2) to handle three obbligato parts correctly and well; in addition, not only to acquire good inventions (musical ideas), but also to develop these well; and above all, to achieve a cantabile manner of playing, the while acquiring a strong foretaste of composition.

Thus Bach foresaw the pedagogical utility of these tiny masterpieces, if not their ultimately universal popularity. The Inventions' compositional ingenuity, their perfect adaptation to the performer's hand, and the gentle way in which they teach the young musician to split the mind between two (and then three) coequal parts—all these factors have surely motivated the teachers who assign the works to pupils generation after generation. But above all, the freshness and vitality of the Inventions, their variety and individuality, their touching grace and naturalness, must have ensured their continued ascendency.

I confess with some embarrassment that, as a child, I myself learned only two Inventions, although for a period I did run through the entire set every day with both hands in octaves to bolster that facet of my technique. But returning to them now in their proper form, with many of Bach's most substantial keyboard works already in my repertoire, I find them as educational and rewarding as I would have if I had given them their due in my youth. The Inventions offer to the musician a lifetime's worth of instruction, and to the student, the amateur, and the listening public at large they can provide pleasure and enrichment without bound.

Principles of Fingering and Ornamentation

In this edition, I have added both fingerings and suggestions for the realization of the ornaments in small type above or below the main staff. Since Bach himself never employed these notations, all such markings are editorial additions which the performer is welcome to disregard if so moved. But in works that were intended largely for students, it seemed entirely appropriate to add a few suggestions that could assist in their re-creation.

Editorial fingerings are a standard feature in modern editions of the Bach Inventions; but curiously, many editions remain silent on fingering in the place where help may be most needed, namely in the vicinity of ornaments. Presumably this silence stems from a reluctance to impose the editor's opinion on figures that are supposed to be free and improvisatory in character. But to my mind, an editor who wants to guide the student's fingers through the scales and arpeggios contained in the Inventions might as well provide suggestions on the more difficult task of realizing trills, mordents, and turns cleanly and idiomatically. In Bach's day, one could perhaps take for granted that students and teachers understood ornamentation intuitively and could improvise beautiful ornaments with little explicit instruction (though Bach's markings, so much more precise and frequent than Handel's, suggest that his trust of the performer was limited). But I do not believe that one can assume as much today, and so for the benefit of students I have added a few marks that accord with current scholarship on Baroque practice and that promote strength and clarity of execution, at least for my own hands. Experienced pianists using this edition are as free to ignore these suggestions as they are to ignore all the other numbers contained herein, although I would still encourage them to consider them carefully. And as my own recording suggests, there is still room to add and subtract ornaments spontaneously in performance.

When adding fingering and spelling out ornaments, one wishes to strike a balance between being explicit and adding so many indications that the eye is assaulted with a mass of numbers and tiny notes. Accordingly, I have added fingerings only where there seems a likelihood of the fingers hesitating or stumbling, or where a particular combination of fingers seems to produce better musical results than the alternatives (which may be more immediately obvious). Sometimes a number placed on each beat suffices to keep the fingers on track; elsewhere, just those notes where the thumb plays need to be indicated. In each Invention, I indicate the notes for a particular ornament the first time it appears, and subsequent occurrences of the same type of ornament can be filled in by analogy. Fingerings are given for many of the ornaments, even those not written out. To assist in deciphering these numbers, they are laid out so that higher notes appear higher on the page. Hence a typical trill fingering might be:

The 3's in this example correspond with the upper neighbor note (the one a step higher than the printed note); the 1's correspond to the principal note (the printed pitch). Similarly, mordents appear as:

Other fingering notations in this edition are slightly idiosyncratic but do not present any great difficulties, I believe. Occasionally, I insert a comma between two numbers. These simply indicate places where the performer makes a psychological or a physical break, perhaps lifting the hand slightly to restart in a new position. In a very few places expression marks are incorporated into the fingerings to indicate the fact that on a modern piano a particular finger may need to play more lightly, or longer, than its neighbors. In a number of inventions, the hands wind up in very close proximity, tangling particularly intricately in Invention No. 2— perhaps indicating Bach's intention to have the works played on two-manual instruments. To assist with these I apply the words *sopra* (above) and *sotto* (below) liberally, indicating which hand must rise above the other.

Other Aspects of Interpretation

As a pianist, I am of course a firm believer in the viability of Bach's works on the modern piano, even though the piano was an obscure novelty during Bach's lifetime, certainly unknown to the composer when the Inventions first appeared. Bach's approach to instrumentation was nowhere near so specific as a modern composer's: he freely arranged violin concertos for keyboard, adapted old works for new ensembles, and even neglected (in *The Art of the Fugue*) to mention in the score his choice of instrument or ensemble. Often enough, he appeared indifferent to whether the performer of his keyboard works used harpsichord, clavichord, or organ; hence to me the use of a fourth member of the keyboard family, the piano, appears readily defensible. The sonic resources of the piano can illuminate Bach's counterpoint and sense of proportion wonderfully. And certainly pianists would be foolish to deny themselves the education and edification that Bach offers.

Articulation is a subject about which pianists can learn a great deal from their harpsichordist colleagues. A pianist does well to challenge the nineteenth-century assumption that the only way to craft a beautiful phrase is to play it *legato*. In fact, countless gradations exist between *staccato* and *legato*, and each can play a part in making Bach's music dance and sing, and in revealing the interplay between voices. As usual, Bach furnishes very few explicit instructions to the performer, and what indications appear give rise to much uncertainty. For instance, Invention No. 3 is exceptional in its inclusion of numerous slurs. By one argument, this Invention proves that Bach himself liked to play *legato* all the time, presumably also in the other Inventions; by another, the rarity of marks like these proves that Bach regarded *non-legato* as the default. Further, on examining Bach's autograph slurs, one finds them very hastily written, and hence ambiguous. In measures 1 through 6 of this Invention, one sees marks that might be interpreted as:

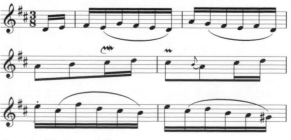

(Invention No. 3, mm. 1-6)

even though most editions (including this one) normalize it as follows, assuming that the slurs are meant to encompass entire measures and that the dot on the downbeat of measure 5 is a mere ink splatter:

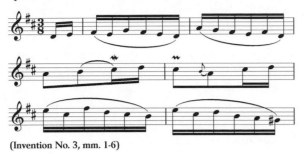

(Invention No. 3, mm. 1-6)

Similar issues arise to a lesser extent in Invention No. 9, and in Invention No. 15, where the autograph of measure 17 certainly seems to suggest the following:

(Invention No. 15, m. 17)

In the end, such controversies will surely prove unresolvable. But I admit that I see a certain charm in the unorthodox readings of Bach's slur marks, and thus I resist any suggestion that what holds in Invention No. 3 will hold in, say, Invention No. 10. I believe that one can add considerable life and character to a line by experimenting with mixtures of *legato* and *non-legato*; the shape of Invention No. 1 might be brought out by a subtle shading of articulation, crudely notated as:

(Invention No. 1, mm. 1-3)

When performing all 15 two-part Inventions as a cycle (a concept that perhaps never occurred to Bach, but perfectly defensible for all that), varied articulation provides an element of diversity, highlighting each piece's individual personality in a way I consider practically indispensable.

The use of the damper pedal is often deemed a great taboo in Bach. I do not subscribe to this view; as long as one is taking the historical liberty of using an instrument vastly different from Bach's, I think one might as well use the resources that instrument possesses. Obviously, one must take care not to muddy the texture, obscure Bach's counterpoint, or produce sentimental effects more at home in late 19th-century music. But light and brief touches of pedal can in fact liven the articulation, highlight significant moments, clarify the meter, and, in lyrical moments, tenderize the piano's inherently percussive personality. The audience probably should not be consciously aware of the pedal's presence, but its total absence is something that I believe listeners will subconsciously note and regret.

Very striking to the student when first encountering Bach's music is the absence of dynamic and tempo indications. While this lack of guidance may be terrifying at first, it can also prove quite liberating, being free to experiment with these facets of performance. Concerning dynamics, I do not, for the most part, find it idiomatic to employ them in these Inventions as a dramatic or structural device in the manner of Beethoven (although a certain buildup towards the final bar can be effective and appropriate). Each individual Invention seems to have a natural level, from which it deviates only slightly. The piano's ability to rise and fall in volume can, however, shade each phrase in a subtler way, just as articulation can. As a phrase gets underway, an increase of intensity comes naturally; even more importantly, closing with a gentle resolution gives a phrase unity and allows the music to breathe.

The choice of tempos is quite a personal matter; I would only caution the student against extremes. The recording that accompanies this volume can provide some suggestions, though I hasten to add that I would never consider these, or any other tempi, definitive. I fully expect that in future performances I will continue to experiment with different speeds, and I encourage students to do the same.

The Individual Inventions

No. 1 (C major). In keeping with its most basic of key signatures, the C major invention presents a quite uncomplicated, cheerful picture, with unpretentious yet perfect contrapuntal craftsmanship. Technically, it is not hugely demanding and deserves its popularity among young students; still, it exercises the fingers most effectively, and as usual the ornaments must be drilled diligently to achieve the necessary speed and grace. When one first views a facsimile of the autograph of this work, it comes as a surprise to find triplets where traditionally performers play straight 16ths in falling thirds; but on inspection one can see that the middle notes in each triplet were inserted into the autograph as an afterthought. Whether the inserted notes are in Bach's handwriting I find hard to judge. In any event, the triplet version is reprinted at the end of the volume as Invention No. 1a. The added decorations, by interrupting the consistent pulse of sixteenths, change the character of the work considerably, producing a texture sometimes swirling and sometimes stuttering, entirely agreeable but in no way more authentic or authoritative than the usual variant.

No. 2 (C minor). A much more complex and difficult work than its predecessor. The lengthy canons and sinuous lines, very reminiscent of an Allemande, must be spun with care, while the many ornaments prove quite taxing, particularly to the left hand. In my own performance I have found inconspicuous pedaling and varied articulations helpful, though both ingredients require a great deal of contemplation. Collisions between the hands are a frequent issue, and I have indicated in several places fingerings that can help with disentangling.

No. 3 (D major). This Invention and the next seem to form a natural pair, both boisterous and rhythmic, suggesting perhaps the festive sonorities of the orchestral suites and Brandenburg concertos. With its frequent and contentious slurs (see the discussion above), this Invention strikes me as having a sturdier, less athletic personality than its twin. The ornaments are quite elaborate and demanding; Bach's rapid handwriting makes those in measures 3 and 45 difficult to decipher, so two alternate readings are given in the score.

No. 4 (D minor). To my mind, a very energetic, even driving, Invention. The various sequences, the many leaps by sevenths, the pedal point trills in measures 19 through 21 and 29 through 33, the note values tied across barlines: all lend the work considerable excitement.

No. 5 (E-flat major). Unusually among the Inventions, this specimen possesses a texture best described as melody with accompaniment, though both hands assume both roles alternately. The spinning accompaniment in 16ths creates a somewhat hypnotic effect. Bach's inconsistent placement of mordents on the second beat of each melodic figure creates a minor puzzle: are we dealing with a complicated scheme, or simple carelessness or haste in notation? I myself have trouble believing that Bach would have been much perturbed by performances that added or subtracted a few mordents by analogy.

No. 6 (E major). This longest Invention is also the only to feature a standard two-part form. Its exceptional grace derives perhaps from the quirky syncopations that alternate with bouncy 32nds and pass from hand to hand. As usual, articulation can make the difference between a scintillating and a pedantic performance.

No. 7 (E minor). Like the d minor and g minor Inventions, the e minor possesses much rambunctious energy; when performing the entire set, one must find ways to differentiate this number from its cousins, whether with dynamics, articulation, or subtle use of the pedal.

No. 8 (F major). A famous exercise for even quite young children, providing as it does outstanding conditioning for the fingers. The buoyant opening subject and the cascades of parallel descending sixteenths produce an infectiously joyful effect, much like what one finds in the *Italian Concerto*, which is written in the same key.

No. 9 (F minor). The moodiest of the Inventions, its lines replete with augmented seconds, augmented fourths, and diminished fifths that would have sounded particularly pungent within the tuning systems of Bach's day. Without degenerating into lugubrious sentimentality, one must create here a mood of intimacy and pathos, and the unusually frequent slurs can help achieve this. But notice that Bach's slurs never cross a barline, and often are restricted to the span of one beat; in measure 8, the right-hand slurs encompass no more than two notes. The variety and complexity of these markings demonstrates again the sophisticated potential of articulation in Baroque music.

No. 10 (G major). Preparation for the Gigue. The stiffest technical challenges arise from the very frequent trills and mordents, over which I have expended considerable effort in finding effective fingerings. Before starting each trill I find it useful to imagine lifting the hand slightly, after which one lands on the first note with enough impact that the remaining notes bounce out as almost automatic aftershocks.

No. 11 (G minor). Vigorous and spirited, Invention No. 11 churns its way through a few basic motives in rapid-fire succession. The pianist's left hand needs to be particularly fit in this work.

No. 12 (A major). This Invention forms a gentle counterweight to its predecessor. The ornament on the third beat of measures 1, 3, 9, 11, 18, and 20 is not easy to interpret—in particular, one must debate how and at what time to end it. The solution presented in this score is just one of many; the trills can last anywhere from one to six eighths, so long as their basic contour is preserved.

No. 13 (A minor). Alongside the C major and the F major, the a minor is a popular choice for younger students and excellent preparation for many of the preludes in the *Well-Tempered Clavier*. The syncopated figure found at the outset in the left hand, along with the ties in, say, measures 3 through 7 generate considerable rhythmic energy. The numerous sequences (mm. 3-6, 9-12, 14-17), often with metrical compression in the final measures, provide a propulsive force that continues all the way to the double bar.

No. 14 (B-flat major). Like the E major, the B-flat major Invention alternates among three different note values—eighth, 16th, and 32nd—instead of the usual two. It is tempting to dismiss the eighths, as in the left hand at the outset, as mere accompanimental filler; but it is important to treat them with respect, and find a convincing articulation for them. The final whole note seems to demand some sort of ornament, whether a trill, mordent, or some combination of the two; but the possibilities are so numerous that I have chosen not to impose any single option in the score.

No. 15 (B minor). When the Inventions are performed as a cycle, this number provides a most satisfying conclusion. One finds in this Invention much liveliness, but also a grandeur suggested by the deliberate eighth notes separated by rests in the left hand, and by the heavy placement of trills every half-bar during the main subject. In measure 16 we work our way up to a sequence (mm. 17-18). The problematic slurs in this area (mentioned earlier) suggest a denser texture, so that, however one winds up realizing them, they seem a natural place to begin building towards a magnificent close.

—Christopher Taylor

Invention No. 1

J.S. Bach
BWV 772

Invention No. 2

J. S. Bach
BWV 773

Invention No. 3

J. S. Bach
BWV 774

*Concerning slurs in this invention, see preface.

**Autograph could be read as:

Invention No. 4

J. S. Bach
BWV 774

Invention No. 5

J. S. Bach
BWV 776

Invention No. 6

J. S. Bach
BWV 777

Invention No. 7

J. S. Bach
BWV 778

Invention No. 8

J. S. Bach
BWV 779

Invention No. 9

J. S. Bach
BWV 780

Invention No. 10

J. S. Bach
BWV 781

Invention No. 11

J. S. Bach
BWV 782

Invention No. 12

J. S. Bach
BWV 783

Invention No. 13

J. S. Bach
BWV 784

Invention No. 14

J. S. Bach
BWV 785

Invention No. 15

J. S. Bach
BWV 786

*Concerning slurs, see preface.

**Or:

Invention No. 1a

J.S. Bach
BWV 772a

ABOUT THE EDITOR

CHRISTOPHER TAYLOR

Audiences and critics alike hail the intensity and artistry Christopher Taylor brings to the works of masters ranging from Bach and Beethoven to Boulez and Bolcom; the *Washington Post*, for instance, deems Mr. Taylor "one of the most impressive young pianists on the horizon today," and the *New York Times* has termed his performances "astonishing."

Numerous awards have confirmed Mr. Taylor's high standing in the musical world. He was named an American Pianists' Association Fellow for 2000, before which he received an Avery Fischer Career Grant in 1996 and the Bronze Medal in the 1993 Van Cliburn International Piano Competition, where he was the first American to receive such high recognition in twelve years. In 1990, he took first prize in the William Kapell International Piano Competition, and also became one of the first recipients of the Irving Gilmore Young Artists' Award.

Mr. Taylor has concertized around the globe, performing in Europe, Asia, and the Caribbean. At home in the U.S., he has appeared with such orchestras as the New York Philharmonic and Los Angeles Philharmonic; as a soloist, he has performed in such venues as New York's Carnegie and Alice Tully Halls, Washington's Kennedy Center for the Performing Arts, the Ravinia and Aspen festivals, and dozens of others. His first recording, released by Jonathan Digital in 1998, featured works by American composers William Bolcom and Derek Bermel. Other recordings highlight the compositions of Liszt and Messiaen.

Mr. Taylor owes much of his success to several outstanding teachers, including Russell Sherman, Maria Curcio-Diamand, Francisco Aybar, and Julie Bees. In addition to performing, he is Assistant Professor of Piano Performance at the University of Wisconsin in Madison. He pursues a variety of other interests: mathematics; philosophy (he has published an article in *The Oxford Handbook of Free Will*, coauthored with the leading scholar Daniel Dennett); computing (one project being to create a compiler for a new programming language); linguistics; and biking, which is his primary means of commuting. Mr. Taylor lives in Middleton, Wisconsin, with his wife, musicologist Denise Pilmer Taylor, and two daughters.

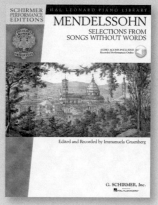